In the Mourning

ERICKA BROADDUS JOHNSON

Copyright © 2011 Ericka Broaddus Johnson

All rights reserved.

ISBN: 1461125367
ISBN-13: 978-1461125365

LCCN:

DEDICATION

This book is first dedicated to both of my children. Aiden, you are the youngest and have the longest way to go in this journey called life. Nothing is more powerful than your thoughts and words. Remember to always capture them.

Second, I would like to dedicate this book to anyone who has ever had a moment where you felt you had no voice…. I pray there is at least a word with which you can relate, that evokes an emotion, or gives wings to your lost voice

CONTENTS

	Acknowledgments	i
1	In the Midnight Hour	3
2	Too Little Too Late	9
3	6/16/08	15
4	Slave to the Red Light	19
5	The Haze	23
6	Separation	27
7	Its All About YOU	30
8	Righting All Wrongs	34
9	Love Lost	41
10	Remember Me?	45
11	A Mid-Summer's Dream	52
12	The Aftermath	57

13	Love's Poetic Justice	61
14	The Forgotten	67
15	"I am a believer in the lighting of candles"	69
16	Untitled	73
17	No Title	78
18	Trapped in a NY State of Mind	83
19	Bejeweled	88

ACKNOWLEDGMENTS

I first have to thank God for every breath that I take. It is truly a Blessing to be in the land of the living! No matter what I go through in this lifetime, I know that YOU are with me. I also must thank you for the family that you have given me.

To my husband, thank you!!!! You have been there to support me whichever way the wind blew- and I couldn't ask for anything more. I applaud you, because I'm not sure I could live with her! (smile) I Love You Timelessly....

To my family and closest friends, I am truly Blessed to have you all. I know that a lot of people don't have families as close as ours, and I consider it an honor and a privilege to be able to call you all my family!!! I can call on any of you and you'll be there!

To my cover design firm, Maples Media Group, LLC, Thank you for your PATIENCE and attention to detail!!!

In the Midnight Hour

Father why is it that I cry,

You've Blessed me so

Needs and other riches

Which the unknowing overlook

You've dotted my I's

And crossed my hooks

ERICKA BROADDUS JOHNSON

True happiness I know in

You I can find

Still earthly happiness

Doesn't seem mine

I know I'm not mortal

But a spiritual creature

And sometimes my ties should

Definitely seem deeper

This man I've got I

Don't understand

At times he's both loving and kind

But coldness is what I oft do find

Sometimes his loves better

ERICKA BROADDUS JOHNSON

Than silver and gold

I'm glad that you've

Blessed me to have and to hold

Will one day things change

Will he come around

Or is this another I've found who seems oh so

right,

IN THE MOURNING

Yet doesn't 'truly' care

I love him, but sometimes

I need to be spared

Please help me I'm

Crying to You for advice

I'm coping please help me live my life

Thoughts:

Too Little too Late

It's funny the games of cat and mouse

From first I saw you

With Kangol and freckles you thought you was cool

I could tell in your eyes it was

Me that you wanted-me you desired

Young and silly I oft hid from you,

You'd come by to visit, your car was blue

We shared a few dinners, walks to the playground/park,

Long talks about backgrounds and moments in dark

Parties in the pool and summers too

It's funny how much I entrusted in you

Yet a secret so precious from me you kept

An adorable life yet I found out through someone else

I guess I was foolish to think you viewed me

As someone who cared unconditionally

Though hurt by your silence I played it cool

For we all have our moments to trust or not to

Weirdly I fell- had fallen its true

Yet clearly I wasn't enough for you

Long after you wanted me all to yourself,

Still hurting I said no threw my feelings on the shelf

I wanted you but feared you'd only hurt me

I knew that road- I'd been there you see

So I said no and you walked your way

Few phone calls and talks since that day

I really missed you I just couldn't say

But in retrospect I reflect, God keep you I pray

Thoughts:

IN THE MOURNING

6/16/08

How do I say goodbye?

I never thought this day would come

So many words so many tasks

But the second's down to one

I pray you know the value of the times we've shared

ERICKA BROADDUS JOHNSON

I really hope the memories make you smile up there

I'm glad there's no suffering for you-

no sighing nor a frown

I just wished I'd known that in

A flash you wouldn't be around

I would tell you that I love you

IN THE MOURNING

And I'd been better prepared

I'd been right there with you

When God called you up there

In the flesh I grieve and cry

While my spirit says He knows best

I just wish that I could still see you

To tell you all the rest

Thoughts:

Slave to the Red Light

As I sit there in

Anticipation of the events

That will unfold tonight-

I am a slave to the Red Light

I dream and fantasize while

My eyes close thinking of

Past times and conversations you see

ERICKA BROADDUS JOHNSON

I am a slave to the Red Light

We shared fluids, talks and pleasureful walks-

Weekend getaways weeklong sabbaticals,

My thoughts were erratical;

I'm a Slave to the Red Light

You see when I'm in the room

Myself and I;

I think about those special guys

IN THE MOURNING

Who entertain me on the Blackberry @ night?

Cuz see I'm a Slave to the Flashing Red Light

Thoughts:

The Haze

Rainy as it may seem

Somewhere out there the sun still gleams

Through all the disappointment and doubt

The Lord's already worked it out

You may have no clue as to the plan

But best believe its all in His Hand

The sun, moon, and stars are no more important than you

He loves and cares about what you do

The path may be hard your enemy's traps set

But the Master is far Greater and Not through with you yet

Stay encouraged and steadfast when all hope seems lost

IN THE MOURNING

You're Covered its Won Jesus paid the cost!

Thoughts:

Separation

I wish I hadn't missed my Pooh

The convo, his voice makes me say ouououh!

The interest oh my beau goes the extra mile

His warmth, his demeanor and umph that smile

I guess that's why I adore him so much

Not to mention the fire when we tend to touch

I love him. I tell 'em yeah, that's MY man

And what's better- God had it all in His plan!

IN THE MOURNING

Thoughts:

Its All About YOU

You don't know how and don't know why,

I've made it through-by and by

The lies you've told the traps you set,

But HE has NEVER failed me yet

Though deeds you do to cause me grief

Always end in disbelief,

You can't see how or understand why

I come out on top in the midst of my trials,

I'll try and give you just 1 clue,

Its less about me and more about you

The one I serve is Merciful and Great

And HE's the one I trust with my fate

ERICKA BROADDUS JOHNSON

Always listening, NEVER lets me down,

When men and friends cannot be found

My Master, my comforter and 1 true friend,

It'd do YOU great good to Let HIM in

IN THE MOURNING

Thoughts:

Righting All Wrongs

If ever the time was right

Or opportunity ripened its now

Taking time to recap all mishaps

Address questions concerns

Maybe even reflect and to learn,

Its now

IN THE MOURNING

My life, your life, generations of life

All solely existing for one purpose

Self serving

When in reality an awakening, discovery

Transcending revelation or

Tranquility need to be realized

Its not about me or you,

More so HIM

ERICKA BROADDUS JOHNSON

Time to get it together

Seek to make things clearer

Stop chasing the material things

People places and dreams

Seem transparent

Listen to reason, wisdom, experience

Seek higher meaning —existence

Draw your inner self nearer

IN THE MOURNING

Time to put an end to the nonsense

And cling to what makes sense

Neither pity nor self righteous

No shame or almightiness

Instead humble sincereness

To learn from the REALEST

ERICKA BROADDUS JOHNSON

The maker and Healer, none

Other is nearer

No Greater a love,

More peaceful than doves,

The answer the way

To get through your day

He stands and awaits only

To commune with you daily

He's the truth and the light and

He turns Wrongs into RIGHT

Thoughts:

Love Lost

After its all said and done

I have lost and love has won

Duped again an untimely trick

Fallen for the power of dick

A show of affection a kiss on the cheek

That shattering feeling that made me weak

ERICKA BROADDUS JOHNSON

Yeah-yeah he loved me he cared

And just like the others he said he'd be there

That was the plan before it'd begun

That I'd learn the hard way he wasn't the one

And such was my fate yet again

It seems like a battle I'll never win

Just when its right it all goes so wrong

Another sad story another sad song

Maybe one day we'll all get to see

When love is the loser instead of me!

Thoughts:

_____

_____

_____

_____

_____

_____

_____

_____

_____

Remember Me?

I'm the one who you said you adored

The one for whom you dropped all your whores

I was the one you held through the night

Who captivated you turning your wrongs into rights

Remember?

I'm the one that you'd crave more and more

The one who snuck you out the front door

It was me that handed you keys to the Lex

The one who you said you could never forget

Remember?

The one for whom you'd write countless lines

The one you said that was "mine all mine",

The one you wrote you wanted in your life

Who in 'The Chosen One', you said would "be my wife"

Remember?

When I wasn't working you'd visit taking and extended lunch

It was for me you bought 12 white roses in a bunch

You'd get out that truck lookin' so fresh and so clean

To go see that girl even though she was mean

Remember?

The one that you said was always so stuck up

The same one everyone knew you wanted to fuck

No one would tame you you weren't playing games

Yet you'd hold me and kiss me you had no shame

Remember?

I was the one who knew when you'd pout

And you'd wonder what it was I was talking 'bout

You'd look into my eyes and get lost in time

I'd love you and hold you because you were mine

Remember?

I was the one for whom you would cook

The one you sometimes could read like a book

You'd always comfort me when I was in despair

I knew that you loved me I knew that you cared

Remember?

I still love you and with you I still share

It brought happiness and pleasure when you said

you'd be there

It's the little things I cherish a smile a light kiss

It's the tiniest of things I sometimes truly miss

You still Don't Remember Me Do you?

IN THE MOURNING

Thoughts:

ERICKA BROADDUS JOHNSON

A Mid-Summer's Dream

Surprisingly

I was caught up in a sudden spinning spiral of

Confusion longing lust and enticement

You captured me

Like walking on clouds

Young love as it was called

Then REALITY took hold

IN THE MOURNING

We'd moved faster than the depth of our

relationship

Passion collided with the

Mystery of our individual

Thoughts and innermost being

Physical vs. Intellect

Evidence of the need for adjustment

Added to issues of compromise

Power struggles like single folk

Oft do arising

Re-assessment what is love

Am I sure I l-o-v-e him

Coping with learning and him

Inside NOT just out

Yet growth and maturity

Took hold, leaving us to blossom

Less arguments slow gradual understanding

Emerging cooperation

Still strong willed yet loving

Compassionate increased passion desires

Thoughts of the future

Plans of what's meant to be

Love, yes I'm sure Love has captured me.............

Thoughts:

The Aftermath

Not bitter

Sweetened

By an unknown source

A redistribution of matter

An awakening of sorts

Past memories erased

Left with only reconnections of present events

Happiness replaces sorrow

ERICKA BROADDUS JOHNSON

Joy leaves distraught forgotten

Symbolism of a new beginning

Now sincere

Pure thoughts and images

Contaminated no longer by the bas been

Only what ifs

Clear images depict new found peace

Wanting rather thankful

For this new thing which has

Replaced the old and

IN THE MOURNING

Given birth to anew

Hope laugher, and love rest

Instead of voids

The unthinkable and unspoken

Manifested itself into

Reality

And what is left

Is a better me

Thoughts:

Loves Poetic Justice

Trapped

Or should I say

Entrapment

Feeling love

Reminiscent of

Old/present times

Qualities brought to light

Sensuality

ERICKA BROADDUS JOHNSON

Wanting to... longing to be touched

Affection always an indulgent smell

You know it

The kind that makes you

Well..

You understand

Aged like the finest of wines

Classy, yet still a little

ROUGH around the edges

Aiming to please

IN THE MOURNING

Whole heartedly

When he's with the

Right one

Oh did I say I'm

Not ashamed

But not freely

Able to tell him what's up?

Troublesome

Maybe change could be wonderful?

On the other hand

ERICKA BROADDUS JOHNSON

Humiliating

What then?

Stuck like a

Young kid needing to

Potty while mom and dad

Yell

HOLD IT!

Its killing me inside

I wanna let it OUT

Maybe he knows,

IN THE MOURNING

Yet teases, tortures me

Maybe not

Thoughts:

IN THE MOURNING

The Forgotten

Unique Sunrises

Wondrous breezes, scenes, beams

Rains nurturing plants

Thoughts:

_____

_____

_____

_____

_____

_____

_____

_____

_____

_____

"I am a believer in the lighting of candles"

Such a symbolic meaning

The flame that lingers

Draws my attention closer

The beauty of the candle

The fragrant smell of

The hot wax melting

I stick my finger in

It drips and then hardens

ERICKA BROADDUS JOHNSON

Forming an off white lump

Which sticks to the side

Of my thumb

The candle represents

Peacefulness in a world that is

Burning with turmoil

Hatred and selfishness

In the midst of it

No one seems to care

Yet the candle continues to burn,

IN THE MOURNING

Beauty and all

Unshaken, unmoved

Undisturbed

Thoughts:

Untitled

Lost in a midst of confusion

Insecurity

Tossed in a world of

Hatred and uncertainty

Life's critical decisions

Hurried,

Demanded shoving away

Others most un caring

ERICKA BROADDUS JOHNSON

And some who do searching for

Answers to life's questions prizes

Happiness lurks within

However, the

Reality must be reached

Perishing the only alternative

Deeper and deeper

You go

Into the darkness/ wilderness

On a quest which can

IN THE MOURNING

Only be fulfilled at

Its end

Seeking to

Find not an untruth

But the promise

Living yet another day

To uncover

More and more

Of the reality

The promise

ERICKA BROADDUS JOHNSON

Unknowing of whether

The end is near

Thoughts:

ERICKA BROADDUS JOHNSON

No Title

Sexy me

Uh no him

Walking with the smoothness

That only he can portray

His skin remnant of the

Batter of that chocolate cake

That you love to eat/ lick

His smile

Reminding you of the better qualities

But beware-

There's more his physique screaming I know you

Want/need to touch me

The kind of chest upon which to lay- feel secured

When he speaks as a man such as he should

A sense of peace calms me? You?

He knows he's got it-

What you're looking for

Confidence not concededness

ERICKA BROADDUS JOHNSON

Admitting when he's wrong

Yet never weak

Gentle and kind

Not submissive understanding

Compromising when necessary

A true man good friend

Chill so to speak

Never easy to break

Yet letting romanticism

Flourish occasionally

Intimate

Yet not overly

Comforting not overbearing

Not outspoken

But when he speaks...

a strong and goal oriented man

My man

My love

My friend

Thoughts:

Trapped in a NY State of Mind

Eyes shut and nose wide open

Distracted and hoping

That a better time is soon

While this unpleasant now is overwhelming

Time warped into the spiraling

Feeling from a dark moment in

Years past

ERICKA BROADDUS JOHNSON

A beautiful moment with my mate

Being robbed by the memory

Of that fretful time when

Not only did you take ends

But dignity

During that time

Helpless, out of place

And miles to go before I sleep

The long ride home my

Chance to weep but not

IN THE MOURNING

A tear was shed no

No mournin' or grief

Now years later you've

Taken my husband's

Caress from me

Smiling on the outside....Dying within

As my present took Exit

And you jumped in

To explain it doesn't

Change it and its

ERICKA BROADDUS JOHNSON

No burden he should bear

So my pen'll

Execute dictation

To help my mind

Change the station

"Til the thoughts

Cease racing

Thoughts:

ERICKA BROADDUS JOHNSON

Bejeweled

Love, happiness, hope

Helplessness, indirect pain

Fulfillment, ease, peace

Thoughts:

ERICKA BROADDUS JOHNSON

IN THE MOURNING

ABOUT THE AUTHOR

Ericka Broaddus Johnson can be described as funny, intelligent, sassy, outgoing, outspoken and a host of other things. But, if you were to ask her, I'm, sure the most important thing she'd want you to know is that she is "a child of God." Plainly put she "loves God and my relationship with Him. I am His child and I am human. So often people equate mention of God with perfection-but for me it's more about striving to have ways that are more like His while realizing that I WILL and DO make mistakes. The key is getting up and continuing on... if I can do that then I can look myself in the mirror every day without regret.."

In addition, Johnson is a native of Richmond, Virginia and graduated with honors from the Henrico County Public School System. Furthering that she went on to graduate from James Madison University where she proudly proclaims to "Bleed Purple". She has also worked in the banking, finance and securities industries and most recently stepped into the realm of Real Estate.

On whatever level you interact with her, be it personal, professional, or through reading you are sure to feel her no nonsense yet free spirit and her what you see is what you get personality shine through.

Made in the USA
Charleston, SC
06 July 2011